IT'S GREAT TO BE A FAN IN MASSACHUSETTS

by Sam Moussavi

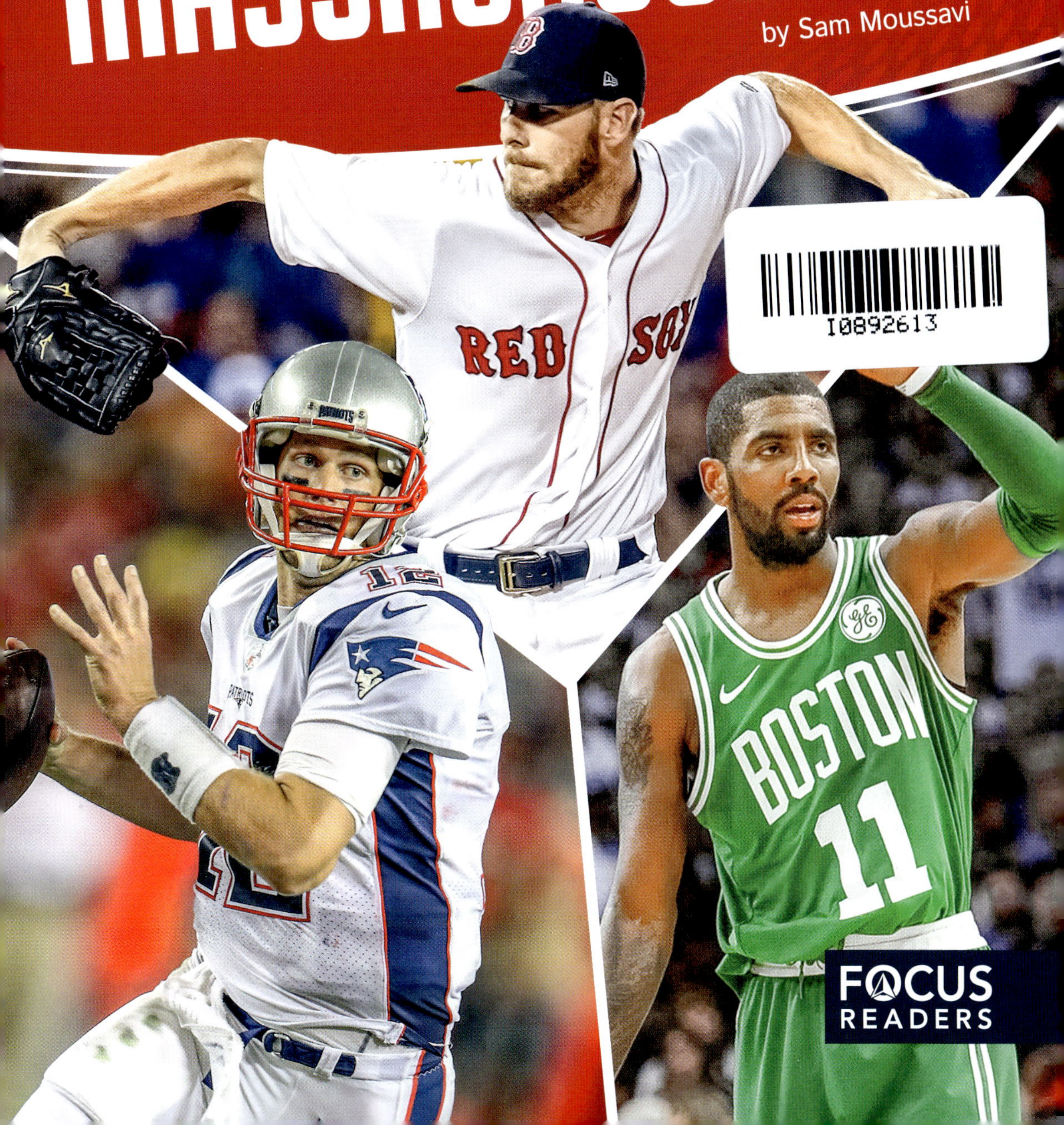

FOCUS READERS

FOCUS READERS

www.focusreaders.com

Focus Readers is distributed by North Star Editions:
sales@northstareditions.com | 888-417-0195

Produced for Focus Readers by Red Line Editorial.

Photographs ©: Michael Dwyer/AP Images, cover (top), 1 (top), 37; Tom DiPace/AP Images, cover (bottom left), 1 (bottom left); Michael Perez/AP Images, cover (bottom right), 1 (bottom right); Charles Krupa/AP Images, 4–5; North Wind Picture Archives, 7; Jorge Salcedo/Shutterstock Images, 9; Jason Tench/Shutterstock Images, 11; George Grantham Bain Collection/Library of Congress, 12–13; Boy Brown/Shutterstock Images, 15; AP Images, 17; Red Line Editorial, 19, 35; Mike Liu/Shutterstock Images, 21; Leonard Zhukovsky/Shutterstock Images, 23; Williams Paul/Icon Sportswire/AP Images, 24–25; Jacob Kupferman/Cal Sport Media/AP Images, 27; Fred Kfoury III/Icon Sportswire/AP Images, 29; Tony Tomsic/AP Images, 31; Marcio Jose Bastos Silva/Shutterstock Images, 32–33; f11photo/Shutterstock Images, 38–39; Winslow Townson/AP Images, 43; Elise Amendola/AP Images, 45

ISBN
978-1-63517-930-9 (hardcover)
978-1-64185-032-2 (paperback)
978-1-64185-234-0 (ebook pdf)
978-1-64185-133-6 (hosted ebook)

Library of Congress Control Number: 2018931996

Printed in the United States of America
Mankato, MN
May, 2018

ABOUT THE AUTHOR

Sam Moussavi is a novelist and freelance writer based in the San Francisco Bay area. He has written two sets of young adult novels as well as many nonfiction sports titles.

TABLE OF CONTENTS

CHAPTER 1

THE BAY STATE

No sports fans have had more to cheer for in recent years than those in Massachusetts. The Boston area is home to four professional sports teams. Since 2001, each team has won at least one championship. The New England Patriots lead the pack, having won their fifth Super Bowl in 2017. But the state's sports scene is bigger than its pro teams. It reflects the long, diverse history of Massachusetts.

Competitive teams like the Red Sox make it easy to be a sports fan in Boston.

Before Massachusetts was a state, native tribes such as the Mohicans, the Mashpee, and the Nipmuc had long lived in the area. In fact, the name *Massachusetts* comes from the Massachusett tribe. Several tribes were living in the region when the Pilgrims arrived from England in 1620. The Pilgrims were the first European settlers in the area. They had faced **persecution** for their religious beliefs at home. So they boarded a ship called the *Mayflower* and headed to America in search of freedom.

The Pilgrims found life in the New World difficult at first. A harsh winter took the lives

THINK ABOUT IT

Why do you think the Pilgrims and the native people clashed?

For a time, the Pilgrims who arrived on the *Mayflower* had peaceful relations with the native people.

of nearly half the settlers who arrived on the *Mayflower*. Native tribes taught the Pilgrims how to plant corn and other crops. The Pilgrims were able to survive and then thrive after gaining these skills. However, the native tribes and settlers often clashed. Over the years, the settlers drove the tribes out of their homes.

For many years, Massachusetts was a **colony** of Great Britain. The United States declared its independence in 1776, and Massachusetts played an important role in the American Revolution. Massachusetts became a state in 1788, making it the sixth state in the young nation.

Over the years, Massachusetts transformed from rural to urban. As it did, the mixture of people changed, too. European **immigrants** entered through the port of Boston during the 1800s and 1900s.

The state's **economy** has changed over the years as well. Until the early 1800s, the state's economy relied on trade with the British. But the United States began to change from an agricultural to an industrial economy. During this time, known as the Industrial Revolution, workers came to Boston from rural areas. They

Founded in 1636, Harvard University has become one of the world's great academic institutions.

sought jobs in textile mills and machinery making. In 1790, approximately 378,000 people lived in Massachusetts. By 1900, the state's population had risen to more than two million.

Boston also became a place where thinkers and artists gathered to discuss the world. In 1636, Harvard University was founded in what became Cambridge. Harvard is the oldest US university.

Over the years, it developed into one of the world's best universities. The school also helped establish the Boston area as being well educated. Many important people have studied at Harvard, including several who later became US president.

The early 1900s brought difficulties in the Bay State. When manufacturing competition arose from the American South, the Massachusetts economy suffered. Factories closed, and many people were out of work.

Things turned around during World War II (1939–1945) and the Cold War that followed. Money spent defending the country created high-tech industries in Massachusetts. Today, the state is thriving. Its economy relies on tourism, education, and health care.

Sports are also a major part of the state's economy and culture. In the early 1890s,

The Boston Celtics are among the most successful professional sports teams in the world.

James Naismith invented basketball at a gym in Springfield, Massachusetts. Springfield is now the home to the Basketball Hall of Fame. Over time, several professional and college sports teams began to emerge, particularly in and around Boston. Many have experienced great success. It's no surprise, then, why fans in Massachusetts are passionate about their teams.

BOSTON

CHAPTER 2

A TOWN OF CHAMPIONS

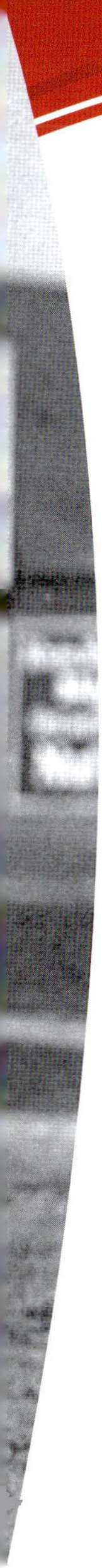

Massachusetts is one of the oldest states in the nation. It also boasts some of the country's oldest professional sports teams. Four major pro teams call the Boston area home. Three were original members of their respective leagues. In recent years, newer teams have joined the older ones.

Boston's first baseball team was the Braves. They joined the National League (NL) in 1876.

Cy Young joined the Boston Americans in 1901 and spent eight seasons pitching for the team.

Over the years, the team changed nicknames several times. However, the team struggled both on the field and in the stands. In 1953, the Braves left Boston. Today, they play in Atlanta, Georgia.

One reason the Braves struggled to win fans was because so many people rooted for the Boston Red Sox. The Red Sox began play in 1901 as part of the new American League (AL). The team was originally called the Americans.

Led by pitcher Cy Young, the Americans won the first World Series in 1903. The team took the Red Sox name in 1908. In 1912, the Sox moved into Fenway Park, where they still play today.

By 1918, the Red Sox had won five World Series. But their fortunes soon changed. After the 1919 season, the Red Sox sold a promising young player named Babe Ruth to the **rival** New York Yankees. Ruth helped turn the Yankees into the

Opened in 1912, Boston's Fenway Park is the oldest active ballpark in Major League Baseball.

most successful team in baseball. The Red Sox, meanwhile, didn't win another championship for 86 years. Fans called that stretch "The Curse of the Bambino," referring to Ruth's nickname.

Several legendary players suited up for the Red Sox during these lean years. Outfielder Ted Williams was one of the best hitters of all time.

In 1953, he finished the season with a .407 batting average. No one has hit above .400 since. Carl Yastrzemski and Wade Boggs upheld the tradition of great hitting. Then a new generation of players took over in the early 2000s. After breaking the "curse" in the 2004 World Series, the Red Sox won two more titles in the next nine years. Slugger David Ortiz led the way.

The National Hockey League (NHL) was founded in 1917. Early on, all of the league's teams were based in Canada. But in 1924, Boston businessman Charles Francis Adams paid the NHL $15,000 for entry into the league. With that, the Bruins were born. The Bruins became the first NHL team to play outside of Canada.

The Bruins played their first four seasons at Boston Arena. In 1928, the team moved into the Boston Garden and stayed there for the next

The Bruins' Bobby Orr led the NHL in scoring twice despite being a defenseman.

67 seasons. The team had almost instant success, winning its first Stanley Cup in 1929. Two more titles followed in 1939 and 1941. However, it was not until defenseman Bobby Orr showed up that the team won again.

Until Orr, most defensemen focused on protecting their own net. Orr proved defensemen could be offensive threats, too. He led the Bruins to Stanley Cup wins in 1970 and 1972.

The Bruins moved into their current home, the TD Garden, in 1995. In 2011, the Bruins won their sixth Stanley Cup.

No pro basketball team has more of a winning tradition than the Boston Celtics. The team joined the new Basketball Association of America in 1946. That league became the National Basketball Association (NBA) in 1949. Two people helped the Celtics dominate the young league. Red Auerbach took over as coach in 1950. In 1956, the team selected center Bill Russell in the **draft**. Together, Auerbach and Russell led the team to the 1957 NBA title. Two years later, they won again. This time, the Celtics kept winning. The team won 10 out of the next 11 NBA titles. This feat has not been approached since then.

The Celtics added two more titles in 1974 and 1976. Another glory era began when the team drafted Larry Bird in 1978. Bird led the Celtics to three more championships in the 1980s. In 1995, the team moved into TD Garden, which it shares with the Bruins. The Celtics won their 17th NBA title in 2008. That made the Celtics the most successful team in NBA history.

MASSACHUSETTS SPORTS MAP

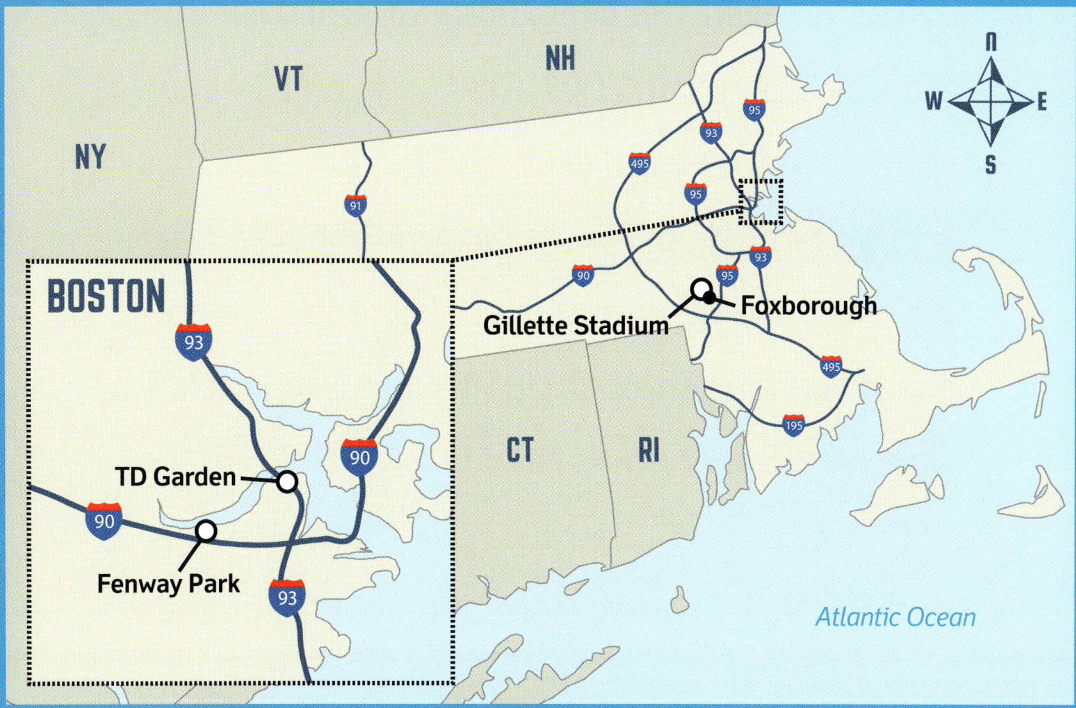

The Boston Patriots joined the American Football League (AFL) in 1960. The team played at various stadiums in the early years. In 1970, all 10 AFL teams joined the National Football League (NFL). One year later, the Patriots moved to nearby Foxborough, Massachusetts, and became the New England Patriots. Now they represented the entire region instead of just Boston.

The team stayed in Foxborough when Gillette Stadium opened in 2001. That year, a little-known quarterback named Tom Brady led the Patriots to their first Super Bowl victory. Alongside coach Bill Belichick, Brady led the Patriots to four more championships through 2018. No quarterback has won more Super Bowls than Brady.

Since 1996, the Patriots have shared a home with the New England Revolution of Major League Soccer (MLS). The Boston Breakers women's

No NFL team can match the Patriots' success since 2001.

soccer team was founded in 2000. It played at various stadiums and various leagues over the years. However, the Breakers folded before the 2018 season.

Not all of the pro teams are in the Boston area, though. The state is also home to several minor league sports teams. One popular team is the Lowell Spinners baseball team. It is a **farm team** for the Red Sox.

ALY RAISMAN

Growing up in Needham, Massachusetts, Aly Raisman knew she wanted to be an Olympic gymnast. She first tried the sport at age two and was hooked.

Aly began training on the senior elite level in 2009. Her tumbling skills set her apart, especially on floor exercise. She also showed great ability on the balance beam and vault. It was little surprise, then, when Aly made the 2012 US Olympic team. The 18-year-old helped the United States win the team gold medal. Then she added a gold medal on floor exercise and a bronze medal on balance beam. She would have won the all-around bronze medal, too, but finished fourth due to a tiebreaker.

Raisman took some time off after the 2012 Games. But by 2015, she was back competing again. By the time the 2016 Olympics began, Raisman was better than ever. At age 22, she

Team USA's Aly Raisman performs on the balance beam during the 2016 Olympic all-around competition.

won another team gold medal, as well as the all-around and floor exercise silver medals. It was one of the best performances ever by an American gymnast. After the Games, Raisman stayed in the public eye. She became an advocate for other gymnasts who had been sexually abused.

46

CHAPTER 3

COLLEGE DAYS

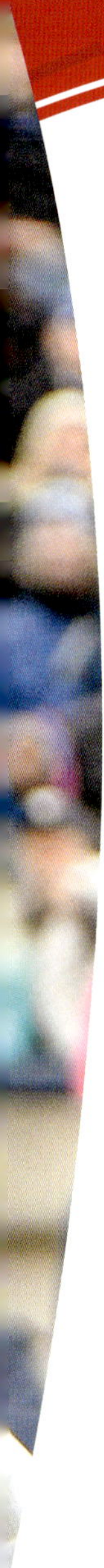

Massachusetts isn't just about pro sports. The city of Boston is home to more than 20 colleges, most of which have sports teams. Massachusetts has seven **Division I** college programs. The state also has five in Division II and more than 40 in Division III.

The state's most historic athletic program is that of Harvard University in Cambridge. The Crimson fielded their first athletic team in 1780.

The football game between Harvard and Yale is among the oldest rivalries in the sport.

Without Harvard athletics, many of today's sports would not be the same. For instance, the school developed the modern version of football. Other innovations include the concrete stadium, uniform numbers, and the scoreboard.

Harvard's rivalry with Yale University is one of the oldest in the country. The two schools have competed in a variety of sports. Today, Harvard has 42 men's and women's **varsity** teams. That gives the school the largest athletic program in the United States.

The most popular athletic program in Massachusetts might be that of Boston College (BC). Located in the Chestnut Hill area of Boston, the school fields 31 varsity teams. Through 2017, the Eagles had won five national championships. All five of those championships were in men's hockey.

Since 2005, Boston College has been a member of the Atlantic Coast Conference.

When thinking of Boston college sports, most people think of hockey. The city is home to four Division I men's and women's hockey programs. They are BC, Boston University (BU), Harvard, and Northeastern University.

Those four schools compete in a tournament known as the Beanpot. The first men's Beanpot was held in December 1952 at Boston Arena.

Then it took place at Boston Garden for many years before moving to its current home at TD Garden. Today's tournament has two rounds and is held over the first two Mondays in February.

BU led the men's tournament with 30 wins through 2018. A women's tournament began in 1979. Northeastern had won a record 16 times through 2018. Locals love the Beanpot because it sorts out the best hockey team in Boston. Bragging rights are on the line each winter.

Smaller colleges have seen national success as well. The Amherst College women's basketball team won the Division III national championship

THINK ABOUT IT

What are some reasons why someone might be a fan of Harvard sports teams? Why might someone instead be a fan of BC?

Boston University's Jack Eichel skates with the puck against Northeastern during the 2015 Beanpot.

in 2017. The Lady Mammoths finished that season undefeated. The Babson College men's basketball team also won a Division III national championship in 2017.

DOUG FLUTIE

Doug Flutie moved to Natick, Massachusetts, as a teenager in 1976. As a student at Natick High School, he excelled at basketball, baseball, and football. But because he stood only 5 feet 10 inches (178 cm) tall, many college coaches thought he was too short to play quarterback. The only Division I school to **recruit** him was Boston College. Flutie accepted the offer.

Flutie played for the Golden Eagles from 1981 to 1984. Despite his size, he proved to be a star. The 1984 season remains one of the most memorable seasons in BC history. Flutie had 27 touchdown passes and more than 3,400 passing yards that season. He also won several awards, including the Heisman Trophy as the sport's best player. But it was one game in particular that has never left peoples' minds.

Doug Flutie brought Boston College's football team to new heights in the 1980s.

BC was down four points with only six seconds left against the heavily favored University of Miami Hurricanes. From just across midfield, Flutie launched a pass all the way down to the end zone. Wide receiver Gerard Phelan caught it, and BC won 47–41.

Flutie went on to play in the NFL and Canadian Football League. However, most people remember him for his incredible Hail Mary against Miami.

adidas
TOLA
T-Mobile
adidas
MEB
adidas
APRIL
adidas
DESISA

CHAPTER 4

BAY STATE TRADITIONS

In most of the United States, Patriots' Day comes and goes without being noticed. But that's not the case in Massachusetts.

Patriots' Day is a state holiday that takes place each year on the third Monday in April. The holiday honors the first battle of the American Revolutionary War (1775–1783). Sports play a large role in Patriots' Day celebrations.

Runners begin the 2015 Boston Marathon at its starting point in Hopkinton, Massachusetts.

The day begins with the start of the Boston Marathon in the nearby town of Hopkinton. Many cities have marathons, but Boston's is special. The first running was on April 19, 1897. That makes it the oldest annual marathon in the world. Today, those in the running community consider it to be the most prestigious marathon, too. Elite runners come from around the globe to compete. In total, as many as 30,000 people race on foot or in wheelchairs. The race is so popular that most runners now need to meet qualifying standards for their age group.

Patriots' Day is also special because the Red Sox always host a game at Fenway Park. This tradition began in April 1959. The game is usually played early, around 11 o'clock, so that fans can get out to watch the marathon afterward. Fenway Park is located approximately 1 mile (1.6 km) from the marathon's finish line in Boston. This sets up a wonderful day for the Boston sports fan: Red Sox in the morning with a prime spot to watch the marathon in the afternoon.

The Boston Marathon was originally 24.5 miles (39.4 km) long. But in 1924, the course changed.

BOSTON MARATHON COURSE

The race extended to 26.2 miles (42.2 km). Today, that is the standard length for all marathons.

Another Boston sporting tradition is the Head of the Charles **Regatta**. This two-day rowing event takes place every year on the second-to-last weekend of October. The Head of the Charles is the world's largest two-day rowing event. Athletes from all over the world travel to Massachusetts to compete. Thousands of spectators flock to the Charles River to witness the event each fall.

The Charles River separates Boston and Cambridge. The course is 3 miles (4.8 km) long, and rowers pass under six historic bridges along the way. The course is one of the most challenging in the world.

The first Head of the Charles took place in 1965. These days, more than 11,000 rowers participate, ranging in age from 14 to 85.

Crowds watch as college alumni rowing teams compete in the Head of the Charles.

CHAPTER 5

AN ECLECTIC STATE OF MIND

Some people refer to Boston as "The Hub." The nickname refers to the city's standing as the biggest city in New England. That means people from surrounding states often go there to visit or do business. The East Coast is also the most populated part of the United States.

This geography has helped Boston develop great sports rivalries. The NHL's Boston Bruins and Montreal Canadiens first played in 1924.

Boston is the 10th largest metropolitan area in the United States.

Today, fans can drive from one city to the other in under five hours on Interstate 89. New York City is even closer to Boston. Two interstates and a train line connect the cities. So does baseball's most famous rivalry.

The Red Sox and Yankees first met in 1903. Since then, the teams have played in the regular season more than 2,000 times. Early on, the Red Sox were the better team. But after the 1919 season, the cash-strapped Red Sox sold Babe Ruth to the Yankees. Red Sox fans watched in agony as the Yankees won 26 World Series while their own team always fell short. During this time, Red Sox fans became known for their passion

THINK ABOUT IT

What factors go into a great rivalry?

and loyalty. They always stuck by the Sox, even through numerous losing seasons.

By the early 2000s, both teams were good. And when the Red Sox finally won another World Series in 2004, they fittingly beat the Yankees in the AL Championship Series. It wasn't easy. The Yankees opened the series with three victories.

TALE OF THE TAPE

Boston Red Sox	New York Yankees
Regular-season wins against Yankees: **981**	Regular-season wins against Red Sox: **1,180**
Best season against Yankees: **19–2 (1912)**	Best season against Red Sox: **18–4 (1927)**
Hall of Fame players: **38**	Hall of Fame players: **38**
AL championships: **13**	AL championships: **40**
World Series wins: **8**	World Series wins: **27**

Accurate as of March 2018

No team had ever come back from that deficit. But the Red Sox did. The victory reignited the rivalry for a new generation of baseball fans.

Not all rivalries are based on geography. The Celtics and Los Angeles Lakers developed a rivalry simply because both teams were good. Through 2017, the teams had met in the NBA Finals a record 12 times. The Celtics won nine of those meetings.

Boston dominated the basketball rivalry early on. The Celtics beat the Lakers six times in the Finals during the 1960s. One of the most memorable periods of the rivalry came during the 1980s. Superstar Larry Bird led the Celtics, and Magic Johnson led the Lakers. The teams met three times in the Finals from 1984 to 1987. The Lakers won twice, but the Celtics won a classic series in 1984. Led by Bird, the Celtics

(From left) Kevin Garnett, Ray Allen, and Paul Pierce led the Celtics over the Lakers in the 2008 NBA Finals.

defeated the Lakers in seven games. The rivalry was reignited once again beginning in 2008. The Celtics won their 17th title that year, beating the Lakers. However, the Lakers won their 16th title in 2010, beating the Celtics.

Massachusetts sports fans are known for being some of the most passionate fans in the nation.

Fans brave the frigid temperatures and snow for December Patriots games. They sit in the cold at Fenway Park toward the end of the Red Sox's season. It's a good thing the Bruins and Celtics play indoors, because it gives Boston fans a little relief from the coldest part of winter.

Harsh winters bring a lot of snow to the state of Massachusetts. As a result, skiing and snowboarding are popular across the state. Blue Hills in Canton is one of the most popular mountains. Jiminy Peak in Hancock is also a favorite. It attracts winter sports enthusiasts from all over the East Coast.

Massachusetts has something for everyone, from the mountains, parks, and beaches all over the state to the exciting pro and college sports in Boston. Sports are just a small part of Massachusetts, though. The history of the state

Summer and winter sports combined when the Bruins hosted the 2010 NHL Winter Classic at Fenway Park.

provides a deep connection to the country as a whole. Some would say American history began in Massachusetts. One thing is certain: unforgettable moments will make their way into Massachusetts history for many years to come.

FOCUS ON

MASSACHUSETTS

Write your answers on a separate piece of paper.

1. Write a sentence that describes Harvard University's contribution to sports.

2. Which team or event in Massachusetts would you most like to watch? Why?

3. Which Boston pro team has won the most championships?

- **A.** Bruins
- **B.** Patriots
- **C.** Celtics

4. Why do people consider the Boston Marathon so important?

- **A.** It is the oldest annual marathon.
- **B.** It is the world's longest marathon.
- **C.** It is the only marathon on the East Coast.

Answer key on page 48.

GLOSSARY

colony
An area controlled by a country that is far away.

Division I
The top level of college sports in the United States.

draft
A system that allows teams to acquire new players coming into a league.

economy
A system of goods, services, money, and jobs.

farm team
A minor league team that develops players for a major league team.

immigrants
People who move to a new country.

persecution
Poor treatment due to political or religious beliefs.

recruit
To seek out new members for a group or activity.

regatta
A boat race.

rival
A team or player that has an intense and ongoing competition against another team or player.

varsity
The top team representing a high school or college in a sport or competition.

TO LEARN MORE

BOOKS

Adamson, Thomas K. *The New England Patriots Story.* Minneapolis: Bellwether Media, 2017.

Tustison, Matt. *12 Reasons to Love the Boston Red Sox.* Minneapolis: 12-Story Library, 2016.

Whiting, Jim. *Boston Celtics.* Mankato, MN: Creative Education, 2017.

NOTE TO EDUCATORS

Visit **www.focusreaders.com** to find lesson plans, activities, links, and other resources related to this title.

INDEX

Answer Key: 1. Answers will vary; **2.** Answers will vary; **3.** C; **4.** A